Read This!

Written by Adam and Charlotte Guillain

RISING ★ STARS

The school librarian, Mr Crystal, needed helpers in the library.

"Would anyone like to volunteer?" he asked Mrs Knight's class.

"Yes please!" said Tess. "We'll help!"

"Come to the library tomorrow lunchtime," Mr Crystal replied with a smile.

They hurried to the library the next day.

"This is where the returned books go," Mr Crystal told them. "Please could you put them back on the shelves?"

The friends nodded and got started.

This is fun!

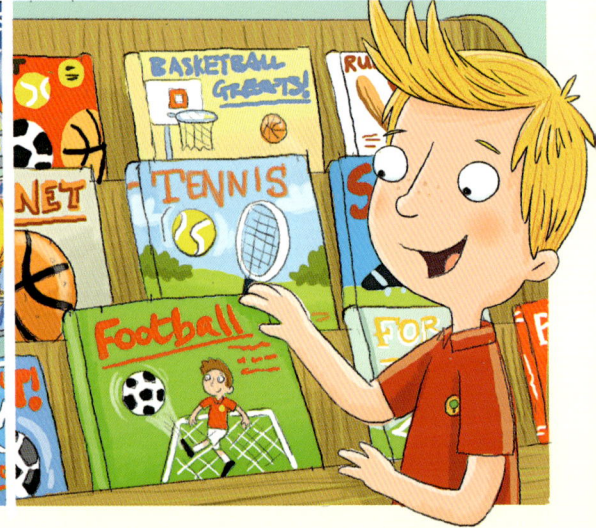

They bustled around the library, putting books away and tidying the shelves.

"You're a great team," Mr Crystal told them.

"I love these books," said Finn as he arranged a series of football books on a shelf.

When they'd finished tidying the books away,
Rav asked, "What else can we do?"

Mr Crystal smiled. "You could recommend some books
you like to the children who come in?" he suggested.

Yes!

I'd love to!

Soon, a younger boy came in to return a book.

"Do you want to borrow something else?" asked Tess.

The boy nodded.

"Read this!" said Tess, giving the boy her favourite story about tigers.

"I'm not sure," he mumbled.

Rav hurried across with a non-fiction book and explained, "I think you'll like this a lot more – it's all about diggers."

The boy stared at the book in Rav's hands.

"What about this one?" Finn said. "It's an adventure story and it's really exciting."

"Or this one," Asha suggested. "It's about drawing."

"The tiger one is the best!" said Tess, holding it up.

The boy stepped away towards the exit.

"I think I'll choose a new book later," he mumbled and then scurried out of the library.

"Oh," said Tess with a frown. "He didn't like any of the books we suggested."

Five minutes later, a girl came into the library.
She crouched down to look at one of the shelves.
When she looked up, she was surrounded by Tess,
Finn, Rav and Asha.

Do you like tigers?
Try this one!

The girl jumped up and ran out of the library.

"This is strange," said Rav. "Why is nobody taking the books we recommend?"

The friends shrugged and went back to sorting and tidying the shelves.

The library door creaked open and two faces appeared.

"They're still there!" someone whispered.

"Oh no! Let's come back later!" hissed another voice.

Rav stared at them and realised that the children outside were too scared to come in!

Mr Crystal gave a little cough. "Do you think they might need a bit more space?" he suggested.

"What do you mean?" asked Tess.

"If you all recommend books at once, children might not know what to do," continued Mr Crystal.

"That makes sense!" murmured Finn.

"We could take it in turns," said Rav.

"And find out what each person likes before we recommend something," suggested Asha.

"Why don't you go first, Asha," said Tess.

Ten minutes later, a boy and a girl came into the library. Tess, Finn and Rav glanced up, but they let Asha speak to them.

"Hello!" said Asha, with a friendly smile. "Would you like some help?"

"Yes please," replied the girl shyly. "We don't know what to choose."

"Okay," said Asha. "Do you like animal books?"

The boy nodded. "Yes, they're my favourite!"

"Tess can help you," said Asha.

"What sort of books do you like?" Asha asked the girl.

"I like books with facts in them," she replied.

"Ah! That's what Rav likes too!" said Asha. "Go and see what he recommends."

Now the friends were taking turns to speak, no one was scared to come in. Soon the library was buzzing like a beehive as children returned their books and chose new ones.

One boy stood in the middle of the library, watching everyone around him.

Rav noticed and walked over. "What's wrong?" asked Rav.

"I don't want an animal book or a book about vehicles or an adventure story," the boy wailed.

"There are no books here for me," sighed the boy, and he headed to the door.

"Wait!" said Rav. "What are you interested in?"

"I like drawing and making things," said the boy.

Rav beamed and said, "You need to speak to Asha."

"You could try this one," Asha said, and she pulled a craft book from the shelf.

The boy started turning the pages and grinned.

This is great!

At the end of the afternoon, Mr Crystal thanked the friends for their help.

"Before you go, could you help me choose the library book of the week?" he asked.

"This one!" they chorused.

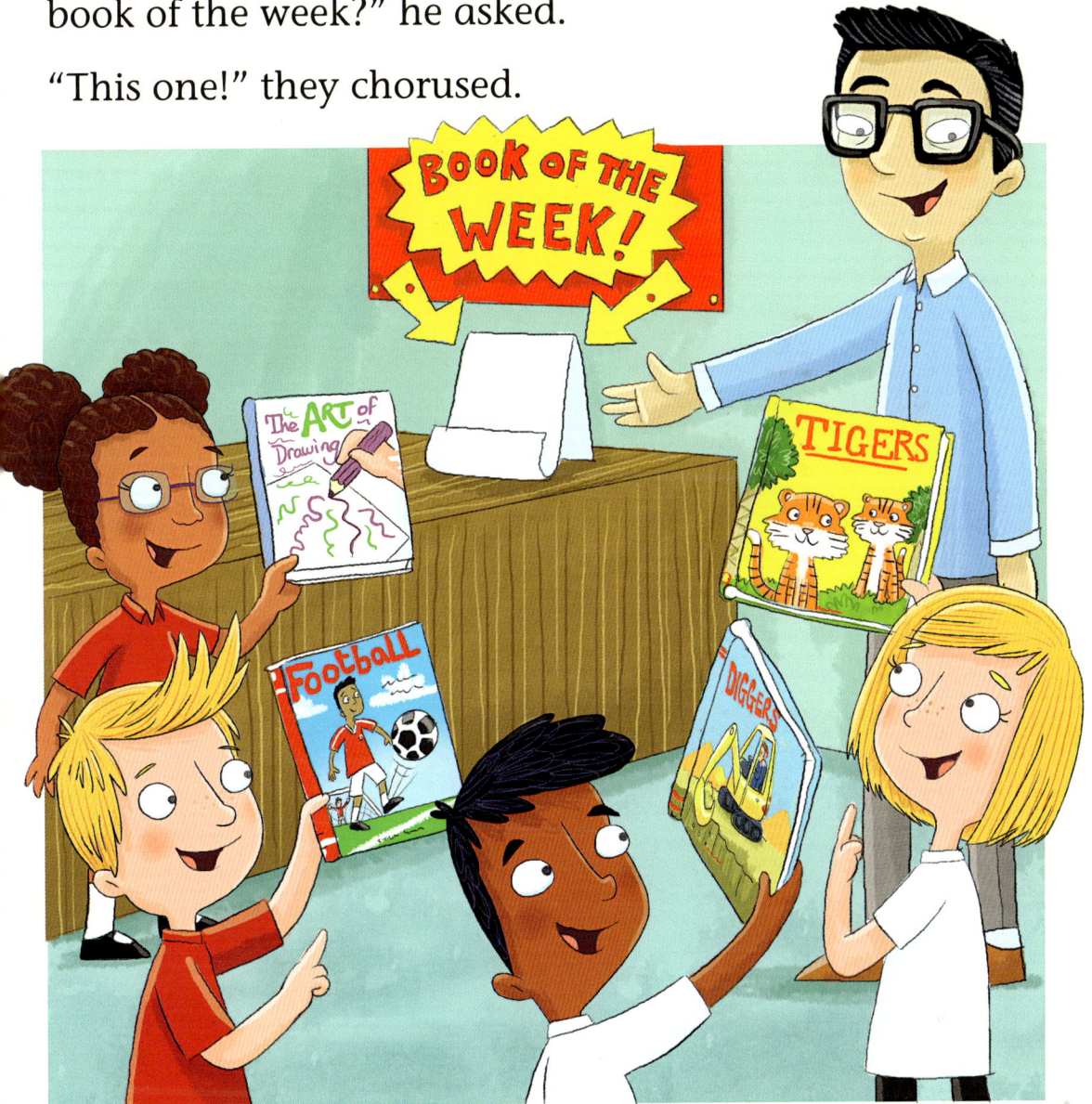

Talk about the story

Answer the questions:

1 What was the librarian's name?

2 What does the word 'recommend' mean? (page 5)

3 What was the favourite book that Tess suggested to the children?

4 Why did the children run out of the library?

5 How did the friends help the children to choose books in the end?

6 At the end of the story, what type of book did Asha find for the boy to read?

7 Use your own words to describe how the friends tried to help in the library.

8 Do you like to go to the library? What is your favourite type of book?

Can you retell the story in your own words?